SG Productions

First Edition 2023

ISBN

eBook - 978-1-7777968-6-0
Softcover - 978-1-7777968-5-3

Cover Image by <u>AlessandraConte</u> from <u>Pixabay</u>:
https://pixabay.com/illustrations/watercolour-painting-art-effect-4799196/

Table of Contents

Table of Figures

What men are saying about A Broken Soul

In a time when honest open dialogue is necessary to move society in a positive forward direction with respect to issues of hate and inequity "A Broken Soul", written by Neil Gonsalves and Brian Sankarsingh, is an important work that probes and resonates. First-hand lived experiences, creative prose and powerful poetic verses combine to challenge the reader to question their own biases and accurately targets where necessary change should be affected. An enjoyable and intellectually stimulating work that I highly recommend. - David Parmer, OCT 30 year TDSB Secondary STEM, Special Education and English Language Learning Educator

Gonsalves and Sankarsingh provide a deeply honest and introspective depiction of what it is to be a man in 21 century society. Caught between the weight of old-world expectations and what today's "enlightened" views now expect of them, at its core it is a rally call, a reaching out to all men for help in navigating what can often feel like a no-win situation. At times dark, its poetic flow demands our attention to an issue seldom discussed and rarely examined. So often lost in the shadows cast by the monumental struggle that modern women find themselves facing, it casts a light on the age old, equally heavy struggle faced by those men who need the time to examine who they are, and then authentically express that without criticism. – Vernon Hiller, District Chief, Toronto Fire Service

Figure 1 - Neil and his father Harry

Dedications

For Harry, my father - from whom I have come to appreciate that manhood, like any other label, is rarely neat, tidy, or monolithic. - *Neil Gonsalves*

For the men in my life whom I call brothers and friends and whose struggles and successes help us strive together to be better. - *Brian Sankarsingh*

About the Authors

Figure 2 - Fathers and sons

Neil Gonsalves is an Indian-born Canadian immigrant who grew up in Dubai, U.A.E., and moved to Canada in 1995. He has been described by friends as a constructive deviant; someone willing to engage in the uncomfortable by asking why things are the way they are with the primary objective of challenging and improving the status quo.

Neil has been a TEDx speaker, a keynote and guest lecturer at several community and corporate events. He has been a college professor since 2006 - teaching primarily in the area of ethics and diversity. He was nominated for the TVO 2010 Best Lecturer in Ontario award. He is a published author and columnist. He has been published as a Freelance Contributor for CBC - First Person and is a regular contributor for Metroland Media Group - Durham Division

Brian Sankarsingh is a Trinidadian-born Canadian immigrant who describes himself as an accidental poet, with a passion for advocacy and a penchant for prose. Arriving in Canada in the 1980s, Brian worked tirelessly to forge a life and career for himself. In so doing, he inadvertently shrouded his love for poetry. Now, with his children all grown up, he has rediscovered his voice.

With renewed vigour and an unapologetic style, Sankarsingh is committed to maddeningly screaming his poetic ponderings from whatever rooftop or soapbox he can find. Wading into controversial topics like systemic racism and politics, Sankarsingh's readers should think about his poetry as social and political commentary.

A published poet and author, Brian also authors bi-monthly articles for several regional newspapers on matters concerning immigrants, BIPOC communities and digital equity. Brian's published books, *A Sliver of a Chance* and *The Human Condition* are available on Amazon.

Figure 3 - The Son of His Father
Lobby card for the 1917 film The Son of His Father – Public Domain

Foreword

When I was asked to write the foreword for this book, I felt shy – an emotion completely foreign to me.

Suddenly shy in the face of such raw, honest vulnerability; in the receding echoes of weighty words welling from depths of deep pain; in the tender wake of … all that …what could I offer, as a woman, in support of two incredibly powerful men?

First, I offer my silence. Not the absence of words, but space for theirs to resound. Wonderful words, clever, literate, wise - tender, broken, simple.

I always wondered what we, as mothers, were doing to the men we always complained about. Women complaining about men as, on tiptoe, I eyeballed the abandoned cookies on the plate between the smiling cigarettes rimmed with red lipstick, while my mother yakked with Mrs. Pye. Women complaining about men as they gathered their children at the school entrance and herded them into the van. Women waiting for Prince Charming in every single story. Women telling sons big boys don't cry. Women saying husband is babysitting his own children. Women chasing men from the

kitchen, extruding insidious control over food, mealtimes, sustenance.

I saw it all. I worried about whether I should – or even wanted to – become a mother. After all, I escaped the family home at 16, clawed my way out of toxic masculinity, toxic femininity, toxic parents – and, inevitably, toxic husband.

One day, I realized I had a choice. I was stronger than all that. Stronger than them.

My son is grown. Beautiful, kind, gentle man, hiding his depression, hiding his strength, towing the line. Despite everything I tried to teach him, the clangour and dissonance outside is louder.

He navigates a world of theys and thems while sucking it up as the would-be provider for a female he's not allowed to approach for fear of coming across the wrong way, in the wrong place, at the wrong time.

If gender is a spectrum, how can we talk about men and women, boys, and girls?

Yet here we are.
Sankarsingh and Gonsalves point out that with male privilege comes male punishment. Disproportionately, men go to jail, men go to war.

They paint the schizophrenic position we put men in - expecting them to provide yet vilifying them for it at the same time: "... simultaneously being expected to diminish and denigrate that role".

Figure 4 - Depression –
Pixabay Free for use uploaded by whoismargot

Critically – for all the gender upheaval since the Second World War when women were called from the home to take on the "men's jobs" – Sankarsingh and Gonsalves point out that: "... our world has not yet created the structural systems for full gender parity".

They ask: What happens when our world loses chivalry? "What pray tell shall we do differently? What new rules do now apply?"

We're in the midst of figuring it out.

Certainly, in the societal gender dysphoria we're experiencing now, where all it takes to be a woman is to simply declare yourself one, it is time for men to be heard in a way they've never been permitted to express.

Jung might say it's what happens when Animus kills Anima. Feminists might say it was the opposite. Nietzsche said God is dead, and most of us are still waiting for Godot.

As men of colour, and as immigrants, their particular struggles pulled my heartstrings through my gut. Canada has an incredible opportunity to do so much better. We can and we must.

This story may have been written about the everyman; but therein lies the heroism. In inviting me to foreword, therein lies the chivalry.

I thank you.

Anna Garleff
Calgary, 2023

Preface

Dear reader,

Broken Soul was written as a way of starting important conversations about men and men's mental health. Both authors of this book are middle aged family men, immigrants, and People of Colour. This intersectionality adds another level of complexity and richness to the dialogue. They have both struggled with finding balance between their own cultural norms and Canadian societal standards.

Some men are not comfortable having conversations about their mental – and yes, often physical, health. This is compounded for men in their fifties, because in their own childhood the norm for how most men should behave, bordered on stoicism. They were raised to be providers and protectors of their family. Emotion was not a luxury they were afforded. This book, however, is not only for middle aged men. It is the hope of the authors, that even young men will find small nuggets of wisdom within its pages. Bearing that in mind, there are several references throughout the story that may be considered antiquated. The following is an explanation of these references by Act.

References in Act 1

Vladimir and Estragon are the main protagonists of the play, Waiting for Godot. This play by Samuel Beckett has most often described as a play in which nothing happens, twice. Waiting for Godot challenges us to laugh at the ridiculousness of the human endeavour and the repetitive and futile nature of our lives. Vladimir and Estragon are waiting for Godot, but in the end he never arrives.

Glaucon is Plato's older brother. He is also a foil to Socrates in Plato's work Republic. It is not lost on the authors that in the Republic, Glaucon is a poet\musician whose own observations and understanding – or lack thereof – of many of the analogies in the Republic stand out.

References in Act 2

Chekhov's gun is a storytelling device where it was proposed that every element in a story must be necessary, and irrelevant elements should be removed. If the story features a gun, there must be a reason for it, such as its being fired later in the plot. All elements must eventually come into play at some point in the story. Some authors such as Hemingway, however, do not agree with this principle.

When the British left India, their final act of colonization was overseeing the split between India and Pakistan which was a division between Hindus and Muslims. This sectioning off land tore families apart and was ground zero for what, to this day, continues to be conflict between the two countries.

References in Act 3

The Komagata Maru incident involved the Japanese steamship called Komagata Maru. In April 1914, a group of people from British India tried to immigrate to Canada. Most were denied entry and forced to return to Calcutta which is

*Figure 5 - My father and me Creative Commons
Attribution-Share Alike 4.0*

present-day Kolkata. On their return, the Indian Imperial Police tried to arrest the expedition leaders. A riot ensued, and they were fired upon by the Indian Imperial Police. This act resulted in the deaths of twenty-two people.

Red Peter is a Franz Kafka story about an ape named Red Peter, who learned to behave like a human. He then presents the story of how he affected his transformation.

References in Act 4

Friedrich Nietzsche famous statement God is dead appearing in many of his works. It is through the voice of the madman in The Madman that brings the statement to life

-

> God is dead. God remains dead. And we have killed him. How shall we comfort ourselves, the murderers of all murderers? What was holiest and mightiest of all that the world has yet owned has bled to death under our knives: who will wipe this blood off us? What water is there

for us to clean ourselves? What festivals of atonement, what sacred games shall we have to invent? Is not the greatness of this deed too great for us? Must we ourselves not become gods simply to appear worthy of it? — Nietzsche, The Gay Science,

Nietzsche proposes that if we kill God, we must replace him. The same goes for patriarchy and we must consider what replaces patriarchy if we say patriarchy is dead.

Brian Sankarsingh

Prologue

Figure 6 - Sad-Mental-Illness Creative Commons Zero, Public Domain Dedication

Prologue

"Globally, on average one man dies by suicide, every minute of every day, yet men's mental health is still one of the most stigmatized topics with men's health." - MOVEMENT FOR GLOBAL MENTAL HEALTH [5].

We all wake up one day with the realization that we have more yesterdays than tomorrows left. The realization is inevitable, but what we do with that knowledge is not. And it has a profound impact on the days left on the ledger.

We wrote this short story to highlight an aspect of midlife mental health that many men struggle to speak openly about. We wrote this short story for the men who relate to the experience, the families who recognize the changes, and the partners who support them. Often, we feel it is "unmanly" to show vulnerability or weakness. While some part of us may know that this makes no sense emotionally, physiologically, or logically, we still believe it. It's been drilled into us by our parents, our peers and society at large for as long as we can remember. As teens, we created a bubble inside us and compartmentalize those feelings. And over time, that bubble solidified was we became hardened into less than emotional beings.

Even though our society's made great strides towards de-stigmatizing mental health episodes, men sometimes still struggle to shed the scripts learned from their formative years. We've even dedicated June as the month to raise awareness about men's health, but an awareness month doesn't erase generational and culturally influenced scripts we've carried from our childhood. We also gave the symptoms outside of anxiety and depression cute, catchy names like "male menopause" and "midlife crisis." But men of a certain age, generation and cultural background still feel bound to the social expectations they have internalized. As far as men's health goes, the statistics are dire: approximately one million Canadian men suffer from major depression each year. On average, around 4,000 Canadians take their own life annually. Of those suicides, 75% are men [1] and more than half involve people aged 45 or older [2].

Experts believe that midlife crises occur in men between the ages of 40 and 60. While a midlife crisis is technically not a diagnosable mental health condition, it's a recognizable phenomenon that triggers new levels of stress, frustration, and uncertainty in people entering the middle stages of adulthood. The concept of the midlife crises emerged in the 1960s. At the time, the prevailing belief was that people reached their peaks by thirty-five, which implied that the years thereafter were a period of decline. [3]

We mean no disrespect to thirty-five-year-olds, but clearly a lot has changed since the 1960s. Most thirty-five-year-olds today are still sorting their lives out and their peak is only a distant aspiration. However, a state of decline is a fair representation of that middle stage of life. We're forced to recognize that we may have lost a step or two along the way. We struggle a little more to do the things we once did. Age brings new aches and pains; an inevitable part of life is accepting that time eventually slows us down. Health issues start to accumulate, the follies of youth start catching up and genetics begin revealing their hidden secrets.

We know as a matter of scientific fact that mental and physical health are intrinsically linked. People with a long-term physical health condition such as chronic pain are more likely to also experience mood disorders [4]. So, at the very moment life becomes more mentally taxing, men's physical health also starts to decline. This obviously doesn't apply to all men—some men do maintain exceptional physical and mental health—but they are the exception, the ones whose feats we see in magazines, books, and motivational stories.

But this story is not about these exceptions. This story is about the everyman. It's for all the men who struggle, who don't think they fit and who cannot always reconcile mind from role. Notwithstanding genetic factors or major illness diagnosis, environmental factors greatly influence mental health in men. In everyday life, the disconnect between traditional masculine norms and the repeated villainization of those characteristics can leave some men adrift. This short book recognizes these struggles.

The American Psychological Association, in its 2018
Guidelines for Psychological Practice with Boys and Men,
made the important statement that:

> *Although boys and men, as a group, tend to hold privilege
> and power based on gender, they also demonstrate
> disproportionate rates of receiving harsh discipline (e.g.,
> suspension and expulsion), academic challenges (e.g.,
> dropping out of high school, particularly among [BIPOC]
> boys), mental health issues (e.g., completed suicide),
> physical health problems (e.g., cardiovascular problems),
> public health concerns (e.g., violence, substance abuse,
> incarceration, and early mortality), and a wide variety of
> other quality-of-life issues (e.g., relational problems,
> family well-being). [...] Additionally, many men do not
> seek help when they need it, and many report distinctive
> barriers to receiving gender-sensitive psychological
> treatment.*[5]

When it comes to men's mental health, our position is
unequivocal: men can and should support men. It's okay to
be vulnerable, it's okay to connect on intellectual and

emotional levels with other men. It's okay to have a network and a support structure to lean on when life inevitably becomes challenging. It's okay to realize that we can't always be the protector, the provider, "the man." It's okay to break the socially dictated scripts that prevent us from being emotive, from being open and most damagingly—from being willing to seek help when we need it most.

9

Figure 7 - On guard, Father and son published by J.H. Bufford
Public Domain

Act One
Reckoning

Act One – Reckoning

"Who's there?"

"I can hear you."

He stepped closer, and I could see him. What an odd sight. He looked like someone from another time. "You waiting for Godot, too?" the man asked.

"No, of course not." I replied. "How did that work out for Vladimir and Estragon, huh?

"You know he doesn't show right?" I added.
"Doesn't he?" The man asked.

"This is ridiculous. Who are you?" I asked.

"Glaucon," he replied "Brother of Plato."

It looked like I'd gone back in time, but that illusion quickly disappeared as my strange interlocutor responded as if he had read my mind.

"No one goes back in time," he said. "There is no time here." He apparently found joy in being cryptic. You could wait for Godot to explain it.

Why

Counting the days, hours, and minutes

Trapped in a time loop, caused by my actions

Should I go on? My heart's no longer in it

I live in frustration, with scant satisfaction

Will everyone see through my illusion?

What will they feel when they see the real me?

Closing my eyes, I can see their revulsion

As they lay their eyes on my reality

Figure 8 - Father & Son Sharing Music Skills
Creative Commons Attribution Share Alike 4.0

Why am I here? What is my purpose?

When does it end? Am I alone?

Why does this feel like an ironic circus?

What will I do when my cover is blown?

"Is that the only play you've seen?" I shouted back with frustration. Yet I had no idea where I was. Lost in space and time, once more.

He broke out in song, "'Bang, bang, he shot me down. Bang, bang, that awful sound. Bang, bang, you hit the ground.' You don't remember?"

A Prayer for the Dying

Ashes to ashes

Dust to dust

I do what I do

I do what I must

Things expected of me

Because of my gender

Responsibilities

Written in my ledger

"Did I?" I asked. "Is this some sort of afterlife?"

He stepped closer, leaned in, and whispered, "Do you see pearly gates? St. Peter is checking the guest list? How about seventy-two virgins? See any of those around?"

"So, I'm dead?" I interrupted.

Where am I?
Hell.
Is it
here or here
after? Am I
already doomed? All
My thoughts and wishes
testify against me.
The pounding gavel

Wake me from my

Reverie

Am I

Dead?

"Well, you sure aren't living," he answered in a matter-of-fact tone. "It's been a while since you did that, don't you think? It never ceases to amaze me how people care a great deal more about appearance and reputation than about reality."

Act Two
Runner

Figure 9 - Father and son shopping in the cooperative
Public domain

Act Two - Runner

Who gets to judge whether Hemingway's love of the inconsequential detail is more realistic than Chekhov's profound principle of the gun? In the theatre that is life, do we really ever have the luxury of knowing or wilfully differentiating between foreshadowing and mundane, inconsequential happenings? That which appears to be background noise and superfluous detail may yet reveal itself to be fodder for the immense fecundity of one's future eulogizer's material. Yet, if it's your lived experience, you will never know how this yet to be told yarn will get spun.

I was born in a place where, thirty years prior, the Muslims and the Hindus drew lines in the earth, managing to do so both literally and figuratively and, somehow, simultaneously. It was of no consequence; I belonged neither to Allah nor Bhagavan. The Portuguese colonized both land and spirit during their short 450-year stay. My tribe would be the Romans, and so I was a minority within my own motherland.

Venture on—across the Arabian Sea and into the Persian Gulf, I now call home a country that had not existed a decade before my birth. The Trucial Sheikdoms previously lived under a British protectorate, so in a twisted sense of irony, my Stockholm Syndrome to that self-proclaimed empire that named themselves Great continued. From being a humble fishing village that dabbled in pearl trading to discovering black gold under the earth, the Bedouin Arab tribe experienced a meteoric rise that is legendary and fantastical. The Souks today are almost like mausoleums of their journey from obscurity to global prominence. The story had yet to unfold, in the grand scale I wouldn't stay there long. In the grand scale, I wouldn't stay anywhere long.

The Void - Beginning

Dust and sand

Within my hand

In the grit and gravel

I've become unravelled

Yet if ashes to ashes

Calms the soul of the masses

Surely dust to dust

Leaves them nonplussed

Alone in the desert

I am omnipresent

Here I sit alone at last

I see the future and relive the past

Frightened by its bleakness

That feed on my weakness

Desperately I scream into the void

Her silence is her schadenfreude

Dispossessed and downtrodden

Will I be remembered or forgotten

As I make my way in the world

A bittersweet story yet to be told

Figure 10 - Father and Son Dizi Tribe
Creative Commons Attribution Share Alike 2.0

During my childhood, I took many excursions to the sand dunes. On one such trip of no consequence in the grand narrative, I ran out into the desert. I'm unsure where I thought I was going—perhaps I was curious if anyone would know that I was gone.

I am here

I am here, I am present

In body at least

But my mind always runs

From that horrid beast

Its pursuit is unending

So, I remain vigilant

My will is unbending

I am ever defiant

You think of the now

I must consider tomorrow

This is my sacred cow

Thus, I show this bravado

Perhaps I was curious how far I could go before someone cared to call out. In the folly of youth, I must have thought I was free. Free from what, though? I had a good life, with good people in it. Perhaps in the imprudence of youth I sought to gain attention? Yet no one knew I was gone, and I didn't tell a soul for another thirty years. "Attention seeking" was not a term widely used yet. Chekhov would want to know if this mental turmoil is the gun that will get fired in the third act.

Onwards, the flight path, a beautiful arc, flew over the great Kingdom and under the ice-covered terrain of land ironically called green; follow the St. Lawrence River over land to arrive to the southern province once called Upper Canada—even though it's geographically lower!

This is home now, upside down, inside out, foreigner and minority once more.

Welcome eh!

Here we don't deal in shades

If you're not white, then you're black

And you bet you'll take that to the grave

Try and unpack that knapsack

We are the conquerors, we set the conditions

We do not need your insight or critique

We do not care about your dreams or ambitions

You are the nomad, and we are the sheiks

Keep your head down, just tow the line

Be a "good Paki[1]" and do what you're told

And one day we promise your stars will align

If you listen and fit yourself in our mould

---

[1] An insulting and derogatory term for an immigrant from Pakistan or any brown immigrant

28

Act Three
Panic

Act Three - Panic

This is home now, upside down, inside out, foreigner and minority once more. I know now where I am, but I still know not who I am. Isn't it bizarre how we can look in a mirror and see an unfamiliar reflection?

Imposter Syndrome

Hey!

Hey you!

Yes

I'm looking right at you

Why are you here?

Were you invited?

Where did you come from?

Me?

Ah

I'm

Not

Sure

You don't look like you belong

You don't sound like it either

We're not sure you could

Fit in

Let's see your credentials

Well!

I did this small thing here

And it's no big deal but

I wrote this thing

And please forgive my impertinence but

I organized that thing there

And made this

I'm sorry

I'm not sure

I

Should

Even

Figure 11 - Father and Son outside Mosque - Sylhet - Bangladesh
Creative Commons Attribution Share Alike 2.0

Be

Here

As if I found myself in a Kafka-like nightmare, I felt an overnight transformation from a functioning person living by my oasis in the desert to a dirty vermin. And, it was the friendliest people in the world who kept directing me back on a boat to where I came from.

Enemy Mine

Is being brown a crime real, or

A figment of a fertile imagination

If it is, what does it reveal about

Racial identity and discrimination

There is distrust of people who wear my skin

Their culture, traditions, and religion

This virulent hate doesn't come from within

It exists to spread fear and division

But what happens when colour

No longer plays a part in identity

Will we realize that we've been suckered

And 'man' can be his own worst enemy

We were at the end of the twentieth century, and yet the imagery of foreigners and boats seemed indelibly ingrained in the North American psyche. Perhaps it was a holdover from chattel cargo or a recessed memory of the Komagata Maru.

My metamorphosis necessitated a new accent, demanded alterations in my pronunciation, and made me hyper vigilant to never be around curry while it was being cooked. The occasional failure to follow the script often resulted in incidents I can only hope my children never experience. They shouldn't have to, though; tired of my cage with no bars, I followed in the footsteps of Red Peter. I watched carefully and imitated my tormentors' social cues with ease. I learned to roll my Rs and stopped calling my cigarettes "fags." It wasn't assimilation for Red Peter or me. Adding an "eh" was simple a means of escape from the cage.

The Chameleon

I've become a social chameleon

I've taught myself to fit in

One might call it quite Machiavellian

But I'm only playing the hand I've been given

To survive in this inhuman wonderland

One learns to blend in with the crowd

But not so much as to lose the upper hand

As to risk getting run into the ground

It's a game many men must play

Made more difficult by colour and race

In public our confidence is on display

But in private our manhood's displaced

It happened for the first time during rush hour traffic on the 401. The sun stood behind me as I edged forward towards the big city. I found myself surrounded by people all alone in their cars, stuck in a solitary state, trudging along to their own drudgery. They call it "rush hour," but the only thing rushing was our minds—our physical self-flowed more like sap down a maple tree. I didn't know what I was experiencing at that moment. One minute I was previewing emails on my BlackBerry, and then the world started moving really fast in slow motion. My chest tightened and I began to sweat. A heart attack? No, I was too young. l loosened my tie and dropped the window. After what seemed like an eternity, it finally subsides. It couldn't have been long. I was at McCowan Road. I don't remember passing Kennedy, but I was only just approaching Warden Avenue.

It was a panic attack, my doctor would later explain. He suspected it came from some buried and unresolved stuff that us products of the patriarchy are not permitted to admit. In hindsight, it's a curious thing how a society changes. Self-care used to be a four-day bender and some dark humour. But we learned from the folly of bravado and created new systems to help. We encouraged men to shed a tear and show an emotion. Somehow thirty years later, we are even more fragile as a society.

Today the legacy of patriarchy is being challenged daily, and toxic masculinity is put on notice—as it should. But, what about all those late Boomers and Gen-Xers who were raised on a steady diet of Yule Brynner, Clint Eastwood, Kirk Douglas, Robert De Niro, and Sylvester Stallone. What about those men whose mothers raised them to "be a man." To shake it off and to man up when things get tough. Men whose fathers worked hard and modelled real-time lessons in stoicism. That ancient path from boyhood to hero to patriarch was ingrained into our internal operating systems. But now that operating system seems incompatibility with social mores. Hemingway knew the subtext matters as much as the text itself, but then again, Chekhov would see the damn gun and anticipate its return in the third act.

Act Four
Manic

Figure 12 - Father and son 1916
Public Domain

Act Four - Manic

Patriarchy is dead. Patriarchy remains dead. And we have killed him. How shall we, murderers of all murderers, console ourselves? That old and established system known to all the world and its people has bled to death under our knives. The Nietzsche within felt a sense of deja vu.

Knives Out

Knives out, ready for war

This is a time like no other before

Murder, mayhem, bring it all down

Remove the head that wears the crown

And when all is said and done

We will find that no side has won

> For monsters we are and thus shall remain
>
> Anything less we shall deem as profane
>
> Knives out, ready for battle
>
> From the present time, since we last ate the apple

Patriarchy's decline in power and influence in our culture can help us dismantle the concept of man, but what of the boys who come next? What new ways of defining meaning and purpose are we to give boys? If the era in which patriarchs were the central figure has come to an end, which human beings will fill that void and take responsibility for positive masculinity? Who gets to define that?

The Void - End

In with the new and out with the old

For too long it has held control

It's time to try a new way of living

We've got to get past the violence and killing

But how do we decide what will be new?

Will it work for me, will it work for you?

We know doing nothing is also a choice

But that will propel us further into the void

It's one thing to tear something to the ground, but an altogether other thing to build something new in its place— let alone something that is ingrained in our collective mores. But beware, nature abhors a vacuum—if not deliberately filled, something will take its place, and that something may just be the devil you don't know.

It had been almost twenty years since that non-heart attack in the car. Life progressed, life partners came and went, and progeny now exists. Over time I have heeded Freud's advice, sublimated baser instincts wherever possible, not perfectly but more often than not, honestly. I played the part, set aside childish pleasures for greater responsibility, been the hero, became the patriarch, manned up, stepped up, stoic and respected.

I've conformed to socially accepted expectations—being the provider, the earner. We seemed to have left that responsibility as a holdover from our patriarchal past—a company man and chauffeur for children. Logic and reason alongside, duty and protection only sometimes seen as toxic—otherwise necessary. Simultaneous the man and demure, the provider and the caregiver. Toxic masculinity was replaced with ambiguity. No longer head of the household, yet enabler of dreams, guarantor of futures, financial planner, and emotional supporter. A modern man—everything and nothing all at once.

Each day blended into the next with monotony and routine. Banal conversations about dinners and cleaning, TV shows with predictable storylines, repetitive, deafening, isolating, patterned responses and socially acceptable conversations. Work and bills, taxes, and car payments. A never-ending merry-go-round with no end in sight. I felt it again—the world spinning really fast in slow motion.

The Rats Race

Caught on a treadmill of expectations
Unable to keep up with the rest
My numbness defies explanation
Even as people tell me I am blessed

I am father, lover, teacher, and provider
I don't have the luxury of making mistakes
I'm told to abhor violence, whilst being protector
This I must do for humanity's sake

My masculinity is derided as a relic of old times

I am told to rethink my words and my actions

But the message is befuddled because oftentimes

The situation is changed and so too the conditions

But where is the real "me" in this reality

What say do I have in my life anymore

My job is to fulfil everyone's fantasy

I have become a magical whore

And what of those who come after me

What of the "men" of the next generation

Will they make sense of this masculine potpourri

Or will they too suffer emotional castration

Men will need your help if we are to survive

Redefining ourselves will be no easy task

Give us your help, don't just break out the knives

Help us remove the patriarchal mask

My mind and my manners often contradicted the perfectly contrived exterior. People bore me and Schopenhauer found fertile ground in my subconscious. Feelings of futility fill a room, and silence can be everywhere, even when the world is loud. Loneliness happen even when surrounded by people. I so became aware and grew overwhelmed by these thoughts. I don't belong and don't fit in. Have I ever? Always the man from somewhere yet belonging nowhere. Still a stranger in a foreign land. Still looking for a desert where to get lost. No religion or supernatural belief to fall back on, the inherent meaningless of human existence being impossible to argue. Arthur may have had a point—is this human endeavour futile?

Figure 13 - Pokot father and son
Creative Commons Attribution 2.0

What was it all for? The books and the paper to hang on the wall. Altering my accent and rolling my Rs. Praised for thinking differently and criticized for not going along to get along. Popular and weird. Out of touch with the modern world? While others seem to acquire knowledge in fifteen second burst, I prefer the rabbit hole through books. Nuance seems lost. Argumentation dead. Dissent forbidden. The scripts written. Conformity is crowned, and the fear of ostracism crippling. I pick the latter, even if at my demise. Frustration sets in, sleep gets harder to come by. My resting heart rate is permanently elevated and apathy metastasizing.

Broken and lost, I can't find my way home. Lost in my head, without a solid ground. Feeling like a stranger in my own skin. My mind is a labyrinth, with no exit door and a swallowing me whole. I've accepted that I'm a square peg, trying to fit in a round hole. I can't keep living a lie like a caged animal in a prison of my own creation. Beneath the surface, I am broken and bent, imperfect, a soul full of flaws. They all like the performer on stage, but this show must soon end. It's time for last call and for the curtain to come down.

I rack it—one in the chamber now. That should be enough, but it needs to be right, a bloody mess otherwise. A drive to the country is good. Home isn't the place for this. Who wants that lingering visual or memory? It's kinder this way, of course. At least, I think. But I don't know. Maybe. Time, too much of it and never enough. A million ideas, the majority left unspoken, rotting in my mind. It was an unrealistic expectation to think they would all get air time. Parked now, ignition off. Out in the middle of nowhere and still the world will not be quiet enough.

I remember the sand dunes from that trip of no consequence. I ran out, but no one noticed. There was no freedom out there—just an empty void with loud voices in my mind. Was it a good life? Who gets to judge? I didn't tell a soul, the answer would have been glib anyway…

Chekhov was right. It's time now.

Eulogy

Oh people,

Shall we together mourn the loss

It's death will come at such great cost

But no one seems to realize

Even as the tears fill up their eyes

Has the night risen on this trait

Must we follow a new mandate

And if no new direction is revealed

Shall the court of public opinion hear our appeal

For if our world loses chivalry

What pray tell shall we do differently

What new rules do now apply

Who among us can explain the how and why

Shall I ignore the need of my fellow person

Will all my actions be seen as perversion

No holding doors, or polite good mornings

Else be faced with dire warnings

Will my politeness be construed as rude

Torn apart and minutiae reviewed

Then as a social pariah and outcast

Would I have finally earned my fate at last

Oh people,

Let us hope chivalry is not yet gone

Let us not quickly rush to mourn

At its heart it demands we be nicer humans

And courtesy is ALWAYS a better solution

Figure 14 - Father and Son
Creative Commons Attribution 2.0

Epilogue

Epilogue

For many men in their forties, fifties and sixties, there is a realization that our speech patterns and thought processes have long ago transformed into a familiar tradition. We are the fathers and the uncles of yesteryear. We have taken their place in social settings that are familiar. We live alongside our own patriarchs, while simultaneously filling that role in many spaces. The wheel of life has turned, but in its turning it has trampled some of us.

The contemporary man is haunted by a strange dichotomy. He is to be both masculine and feminine; both provider and caregiver; both rational and emotional; both stoic and vulnerable; both provider and reformer. He is to condemn the traditional man, the exemplar of 'toxic masculinity' and espouse the virtue of the modern man who must abhor masculine scripts of earlier generations. Yet this was his upbringing, his conditioning, his tutelage throughout life both consciously and subconsciously.

The story and the poetry contained in this book were intended to draw attention to the inner workings that may haunt some men. It tries to play out the inner tension that many men face; where they are unsure whether to step forward or stay back; where they struggle to find their voice without inadvertently offending anyone because of their privilege. Yet, it is this very privilege that is stifling them; choking their creativity like a tyrannical overlord. Still, society is not made up of absolutes and as such this is not a definitive statement on the state of manhood writ large, but provides recognition to the gaps that exist, the void that permeates and the ambiguity that characterizes the life of some many men of a certain age and culture.

The social fabric of our world has not yet created the structural systems for full gender parity. These facts are evident in the activism that seeks to end gendered wage gaps and career inequities. While noble in their pursuit, this activism leaves a large swath of men in the precarious position of accepting their own phasing out. Until perfect harmony between the genders is full realized, however, men still disproportionately represent the primary earners in the household. That is a double-edged sword; it creates pressures to conform to by-gone scripts related to the role of provider, while simultaneously being expected to outwardly diminish and denigrate that very role in society.

Whether or not these views are widely supported by evidence, they have a perceptual impact on the lived experiences of men caught in the middle. We, the authors of this book are of Indian ancestry; one whose family for generations has made the West Indies home, the other from the old motherland untethered only as recently as the 1970s. Both are Gen. X-ers who categorically share more in common with Boomers than even to the oldest Millennials. And both come from cultures that valued silent stoicism over emotional expression. While we raise our respective children with contemporary interpretations, we routinely judge ourselves by the mores of our cultural programming—that, at times, can be downright exhausting.

There are benefits to accepting these realities. There is significant social and psychological value to embracing the company and fellowship of other men whose experiences help them relate. There is value in positive masculinity, and there is room still for good men everywhere. The bond of friendship between the authors is what inspired them to share collaborative space, support each other's creativity and fulfill a sense of brotherhood through counsel and confidence. When the weight of the world appears to be pushing down on your shoulders, when the contradictions of contemporary life create loneliness and melancholy, when feeling misunderstood is just familiar, the hand of a brother can help.

Our mental health services may have backlogs, the system may not always be prompt and efficient, but positive camaraderie can offer a lifeline when you need it most. It's okay to not always be okay and finding help that works is sometimes a process. Ironically, at your most vulnerable you

need to find a little bit of that old school stoicism, if for no
other reason than to keep you in the fight.

Mental Health Resources in Ontario

Government of Canada

Free and confidential mental health and substance use support is available 24 hours a day, 7 days a week from Wellness Together Canada. This is a Government of Canada website that provides a list of mental health resources sorted by province. It also provides a hotline for Wellness Canada https://www.canada.ca/en/public-health/services/mental-health-services/mental-health-get-help.html

Scan the QR code to go to this website

Government of Ontario

Mental health is just as important as physical health. Learn about supports available to you, and how to get help when you need it.

https://www.ontario.ca/page/find-mental-health-support

Scan the QR code to go to this website

References

1. https://homewoodhealth.com/corporate/blog/mens-mental-healthhttps://www.camh.ca/en/driving-change/the-crisis-is-real/mental-health-statistics

2. https://www.camh.ca/en/driving-change/the-crisis-is-real/mental-health-statisticshttps://www.choosingtherapy.com/midlife-crisis-in-men/

3. https://www.choosingtherapy.com/midlife-crisis-in-men/#:~:text=Experts%20believe%20that%20midlife%20crises,ages%20of%2040%20and%2060.&text=The%20timing%20of%20one's%20midlife,as%20someone%20who%20is%2063.

4. https://www.camh.ca/en/driving-change/the-crisis-is-real/mental-health-statistics

5. https://www.thedotcanada.ca/blog-mental-health-ontario-canada/men-and-mental-health

Acknowledgments

Special thanks to Anna Garleff for writing the foreword for this book. Her friendship, support and contribution is greatly appreciated.

Anna Garleff Bio:

Anna Garleff is an Organizational Psychologist and Executive Coach with more than twenty years of international experience in the design and implementation of corporate strategy and communications. In addition to ghostwriting for Big Four's

Figure 15 - Anna Garleff

such as KPMG, Deloitte, and PwC, she has also provided strategic and tactical support for non-profits and start-ups.

She is the former Director of the Open University (UK) operations in Germany; responsible for the recruitment, marketing, and retention strategies across northern Europe. Anna has worked with organizations such as CRIEC (Calgary Region Immigrant Employment Council), AIMGA (Alberta International Medical Graduates Association), and Hive Mind Network (UK), providing boutique executive coaching and consulting services for clients and C-Suite leaders in Calgary, and around the world.

Her work was commended by the former Minister of Environment, Shannon Phillips. Previous work includes Leaders Developing Leaders Program for the Calgary Fire Department; MBTI assessments and coaching for C-suite executive leaders; and Leadership Training for members of the European Parliament.

Notably, she co-founded two major centres of excellence: The European Centre For Antizyganism Research, and The Alberta Renewable Energy Alliance, which looked specifically into hydrogen and other renewable energy sources. It was the start of the "sustainability movement" in the province of Alberta.

Anna has lived and worked in a number of countries around the world, learning languages from the ground up, raising a child in a foreign culture, and going through harrowing immigration processes. None were as difficult as repatriating to Canada, and this is why she volunteers so much of her time to helping newcomers.

Seeking Veritas by The Professor, The Poet, & Friends

See more from the authors on their substack publication, seeking veritas, by the professor, the poet, and friends at

sgproductions.substack.com

Scan the QR code to go to this website

Seeking Veritas by The Professor, The Poet & Friends represents an amalgamation of our writings, musings, and attempts at honest discourse. We share original social commentary, poetry, and creative contributions by collaborating writers we endearingly refer to as Friends! - We showcase the work of multiple writers in an attempt to support and build each other up.

Why Now? Why Us?

Figure 17 - Brian Sankarsingh (l) and Neil Gonsalves (r)

The two of us met quite serendipitously in the spring of 2022. We were both looking for ways to give back and build community around a shared passion for writing. Individually, we found a non-profit organization that presented a veneer of noble intent and progressive thought. Unfortunately, as is often the case, we soon discovered all that glittered there was anything but gold. This setback left us with a void and an unresolved yearning to contribute to the Canadian creative and literary landscape. Without an organization to belong to, we found value in each other's company over breakfast meetings. We discussed book, blog, and theatrical play ideas—and just about anything else our "Yes, and..." attitude would permit.

Before we knew it, napkin notes no longer sufficed. We required notepads and tablets to keep track of our wonderful conversations and the unfettered creativity that kept the restaurant from turning over our table in a timely fashion. From our early conversations, it became evident we shared a deep-rooted desire to highlight the value of diversity of thought and the importance of intellectual curiosity. And over the course of many breakfast meetings, we found common ground—common ground in our willingness to challenge the status quo and push the boundaries of acceptable discourse. We believe that by doing so, we can better celebrate differences while appreciating our common humanity. Through our conversations, we sought a way to build upon the benefits of including varied perspectives. Our little community of two quickly became our creative outlet, a space where, despite our differences, a professor and a poet could engage in civil debate, find common ground, and show mutual respect.

Our mediums undoubtedly differ, our thoughts diverge often, and yet we find convergence through our shared commitment to cooperation and understanding. Somewhere along the way, we realized that we wanted to share this positive and healthy space with other like-minded individuals. We knew it takes a community to develop truly lasting, meaningful change, so we moved forward to make that vision a reality. We registered Sankarsingh-Gonsalves Productions as a small Ontario business, but we decided to stay clear of the pressure most startups face—to see a return on investment within the first eighteen months. We are both fortunate to have full-time day jobs in fields that satisfy us and, from a practical perspective, keep the lights on. Brian works in healthcare and Neil in post-secondary teaching. This endeavour, then, in its truest sense, is a labour of love, a community of hope and a place where creativity can be unleashed.

Perhaps someday we will leave the sole proprietorship structure behind. If we do, it will be to invest our time, energy, and commitment to founding a non-profit organization whose ethics and values reflect the sincerity of our commitment: to hone our craft and help new and emerging word artists in sharing their voice widely and proudly. Until then, we are co-authoring a book aptly titled 'The Professor & the Poet,' we are co-writing a play and building an archive of original content to share with other thirsty travellers following the route of social knowledge. Perhaps some of you will see a common cause and join us in this community-building endeavour. We want to create a community that celebrates the myriad of ways humans live, think, and express themselves. We would love for you to be a part of this journey.

But this begs the question: why build this community? Why now? Why us? We set out to answer two different questions: if not now, then when? And if not this, then what? It turns out that a great deal of our fears lay in that ubiquitous, self-imposed barrier known as imposter syndrome. We both have spent so much time staring at the mirror of self-doubt, wondering why anyone would want to read our work and share our vision, that we have, for some time, lost sight of our "why." But this is no more. Why now? Why us? Simply, we are two men tip toeing closer to retirement looking for ways to keep the joy in our respective lives. Our "why" is simple: we love to think, we love to write, and we love to share. It was about time to stop letting perfection be the enemy of the good. It was time to take down that mirror of self-doubt and try something new. It was time to respond, why not now? And why not us?

This project is us applying what we have, for decades, told our students and employees in classrooms and boardrooms. To dare greatly, to fail forward, to dream, to pursue, to live, and to learn. This project is us taking the first step in the journey of a thousand miles. If we fail, we will fail forward and learn something. If we only gain a few followers, we will look back at this project as time well spent because we will have written these words presently locked inside our minds.

Figure 18 - CL Society 210 Father and son
Creative Commons Attribution 2.0

If this community does not grow as much as we would like, we will still have made a few new friends along the way. And if our pocket books do not grow, then at least our inner writer's souls will have been enriched. Neither one of us is completely sure about how our respective wives will take the last line, but come along for the ride and, for better or worse, you might find out!

The Professor & the Poet by Brian Sankarsingh

The Professor and the Poet

Side by side, each deep in thought

Lost in their worlds

The Professor pondered theories,

philosophy and facts

The Poet dreamed of rhymes and verse,

the beauty of words and acts

But as they began to talk

They found some common ground

The Professor loved the beauty of truth

And the Poet the truth of beauty

They spoke of the world and its ways

The many mysteries that lay within

They laughed and cried and shared

Of their lives, their thoughts, and kin

And as their days came to a close

As the sun began to set

The Professor and the Poet realised

They were not so different yet

For though their paths in life did differ

Their hearts did beat together

The love of knowledge and beauty

United them forever

Collaborate with Us

Figure 19 - The Professor and The Poet Seeking Veritas

Are you an aspiring writer? Would you like to work with us and bring your ideas to life? Contact us and pitch your ideas, we are always looking for talented and creative people to collaborate with as we grow our writing community.

Co-Owners Brian Sankarsingh and Neil Gonsalves can be

reached by email at:

brian@sgproductions.ca

neil@sgproductions.ca

Website: www.sgproductions.ca

Scan the QR code to go to this website

About the Editors

Poetry edited by **<u>Jayson Sankarsingh</u>**

Jayson-Tyler Sankarsingh is a published poet originally from Calgary, Alberta and currently residing in Stouffville, Ontario. Starting his journey in poetry from a young age, one of his poems on the 2010 Copiapó Mining Incident was featured in the Chilean cabinet. Jayson has

Figure 20 - Jayson-Tyler Sankarsingh

since gone on to attend McMaster University, graduating with a BA in Political Science in 2019.

Leandre Larouche of Trivium Writing Inc.

Figure 21 - Leandre Larouche

Leandre is a Canadian author, editor, and writing coach originally from the province of Quebec. He has lived, studied, and worked in Canada, the U.S., and the U.K. At the age of 21, he published his first book, and then completed studies in English literature and professional writing. His work as a writing coach and editor led him to develop a proprietary writing method, *The Architecture of Writing*. Today he is the president and owner of Trivium Writing Inc., an education business dedicated to writing.

Beneficiaries

The authors have pledged to donate 50% of all year one book sales to a registered charity that focuses on men's mental health. Follow us on social media for updates.

LinkedIn

Scan the QR code to go to this website

Facebook

Scan the QR code to go to this website